THE ZEN OF FARTING

If you want eternal bliss,
You gotta cut the Swiss.

THE ZEN *of* FARTING

TEACHINGS FROM
THE FIRST ZEN MASTER

Reepah Gud Wan

BY A DISCIPLE

Frog Books
Berkeley, California

Enthea Press
Atlanta, Georgia

Published by
Enthea Press, P.O. Box 297
Marble Hill, Georgia 30148

and Frog Books, an imprint of
North Atlantic Books
P.O. Box 12327
Berkeley, California 94712

Illustrations by Harry S. Robins
Cover and book design by Maxine Ressler

Printed in the United States of America

The Zen of Farting is sponsored and published by the Society for the Study of Native Arts and Sciences (dba North Atlantic Books), an educational nonprofit based in Berkeley, California, that collaborates with partners to develop cross-cultural perspectives, nurture holistic views of art, science, the humanities, and healing, and seed personal and global transformation by publishing work on the relationship of body, spirit, and nature.

North Atlantic Books' publications are available through most book-stores. For further information, call 800-733-3000 or visit our website at www.northatlanticbooks.com.

ISBN-13: 978-1-58493-085-3

Library of Congress Cataloging-in-Publication Data

Japikse, Carl.
    The Zen of farting / by Carl Japikse ; illustrations by Harry S. Robins.– 2nd ed.
        p. cm.
    ISBN 1-58394-085-5
    1. Herrigel, Eugen, 1884-1955–Parodies, imitations, etc. 2. Zen Buddhism–Humor. 3. Flatulence–Humor. I. Title.
    PN6231.P3J35 2003
    818'.5402–dc21

                                                2003004834

3 4 5 6 7 8 UNITED 18 17 16 15

Printed on recycled paper

... When my Julia breaks her wind,
     There issues from her fair behind
A breath that would become, I ween,
     A Pallas or a Paphian Queen;
No hollow clamor speaks the birth
     Of this ethereal child of earth,
But hot and swift it mounts the air,
     Dispensing savour everywhere;
Swooning with ecstacy, I kiss
     The heaven that breathed this
          gale of bliss.

—*Eugene Field*
A parody of Robert Herrick

CONTENTS

Dedicated to
Jared Edward Day,
A fartist of great talent
whose rendition of
"The Theme from Jeopardy"
blew us all away

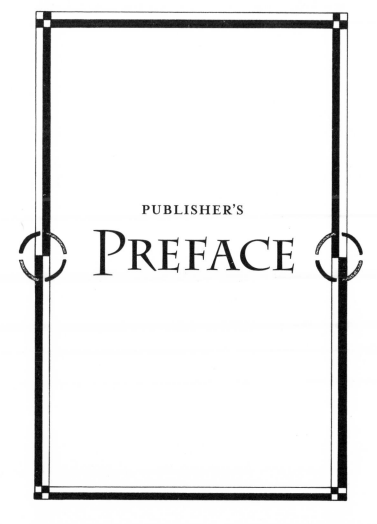

PUBLISHER'S

PREFACE

At first blush, it must seem unbearably demeaning for Zen—however you may interpret the word—to be associated with anything so vulgar as flatulence. Even if you make a major concession, and agree that farting is a perfectly natural function, you might still think that the practice of Zen and the habit of letting one fly are poles apart. You may therefore be tempted to believe that either this is all just a crude, perhaps even malicious, joke—or that there is a deep mystery hidden in flatulence, a certain aura surrounding the subject, that has hitherto escaped the attention of Western science, which thinks it knows everything. Perhaps you are one of the millions who find anything like Zen to be somewhat exotic and somehow beguiling, probably filled with arcane secrets that could improve your life immeasurably, if only the truth were known.

This little book about Zen will indeed reveal the truth about this legendary practice. It would not be wise, however, to entertain Great Expectations about uncovering any deep mystical secrets. Zen has never hidden any mystical truths or forbidden knowledge. As you will discover, Zen does not even understand itself— or its true heritage. It is a strange, even bizarre, history.

The story begins almost six years ago. I was going through the mail that any publisher receives, including the daily avalanche of query letters and sample chapters from wannabee writers who are convinced that they have written the great American novel—or the best poetry since Colley Cibber. Most books that are published today are not well written, let alone the ones that never emerge from the chrysalis stage of a typed manuscript. But nothing can halt the

Great Deluge, and the manuscripts keep coming. Modern word processing only makes it easier—and affordable—for all of these dilettante Dylans—that's Thomas, not Bob—to pursue the craft of writing as though it were psychotherapy.

In any event, I was reading my junk mail, when I came across a packet postmarked in an obscure village in Taiwan. The notion that someone living in a fishing village on the coast of Taiwan might have written a manuscript with the idea of turning it into a book intrigued me. I had never published a book on the mating instincts of Oriental fish before, but why not? I am as open-minded as any editor.

So I tore into the packet, and pulled out three items. One was a very old scroll made of tattered rice paper, written in the characteristic glyphs of the Chinese tongue. The other two were neatly typewritten pages on modern paper. In English. The one, I gathered, was a translation of the rice paper scroll. The second was a lengthy explanation of the scroll, addressed to me. I reproduce this explanation here in full:

"Allow me to introduce myself. I am Lett Wan Fli, a direct lineal descendent of a Buddhist monk who lived twelve hundred years ago. I am not a practicing Buddhist; I am a fisherman who thinks little of anything except the weather, the sea, my boat, and the fish.

"Earlier this year, an ancient chest that has been in our family for hundreds of years was presented to me by my father, just before he died. I asked him what the chest contained. He answered that he did not know; he had never been interested in it. He had received it from his father in much the same way that I was now receiving it, but he had not asked for it. He regarded the chest as something akin to your tradition of Pandora's box; if he ever opened it, only the gods know what misfortune might befall us.

"'Could it not be a good fortune, O honored father?' I asked.

"'Good fortune comes from the sea, my son—not from chests.' It was obvious that he had never heard of Dolly Parton.

"In asking other family members and consulting written family records, I have since learned that the chest had probably not been opened in at least three hundred years. I could not understand why a family would be so indifferent to something so provocative, mysterious, and ineffable as the chest. So, a few weeks after we cremated my father and cast his ashes into the sea, I picked the lock on the chest.

"The only thing inside was the scroll that I am forwarding to you. I hope that you will handle it carefully—it is very fragile—and it has great value to us. It was written by my great ancestor, Pin-Chee Wan, the brother and disciple of the Buddhist master Reepah Gud Wan, more than twelve hundred years ago.

"The legacy of Reepah Gud Wan has been lost to time. Only my family continues to know today who he was. But even we did not have any grasp of the role he played in the life, culture, and history of our esteemed neighbor, Japan.

"Reepah Gud Wan is responsible for Zen.

"When I first opened the chest and learned this fact, I burst with pride. Now, however, I am equally beset with shame, for I have come to understand how right the Master was. Japan was not ready for Buddhism. They missed the point of Zen completely. Here is the proof.

"My ancestors, Reepah Gud Wan and Pin-Chee Wan, lived on mainland China at the time of the Deng Dynasty. Both were practicing Buddhists. Reepah had spent twenty years in India and Ceylon, where he had learned all of the teachings and practices of Buddhism. He had returned to China to teach his countrymen the way out of suffering. But shortly after his return, he had a dream as he slept. In the dream, the Buddha himself appeared to Reepah and asked him to take his teachings to the people of Japan, a war-like, competitive people who had become stifled by ancient religious traditions.

"When he awoke, Reepah knew what he had to do. He arranged passage by boat to the islands of Japan, and departed on his journey that very same day.

"Our family did not see Reepah again for seven years, when he returned. He was deeply discouraged. The Japanese, it turned out, had been eager to learn Buddhism and respectful of its traditions, but they had a hard time mastering its subtleties. They wanted to reduce the teachings of Gautama to formulas and rituals.

"'They will sit all day in the correct asana,' Reepah would say, 'but at the end of the day, they are no closer to enlightenment than they were at the beginning. They are too absorbed in their old habits and ways. I have not had any success at all—and yet my students think they are doing wonderfully well! They all believe they are storming the gates of Paradise!'

"He had not given up; he had just come home to collect his thoughts and plan a new approach. He reflected upon his dilemma for hours every day; eventually, he achieved a breakthrough.

"'The problem with my students,' he said to his brother, Pin-Chee, 'is that they take themselves far too seriously. They do not laugh.

Everything is a matter of life or death to them. They must lighten up and discover some joy. This is what I shall do.'

"He proceeded to outline his plan to teach his students a system he called 'Zen,' based on a Buddhist proverb: 'that which does not nourish you must be expelled.' Just as the expulsion of rectal odors is referred to by you as 'farting,' in ancient Senzar, the language of the gods on which Sanskrit is based, flatulence is commonly known as zend. In fact, it is the original root for your English word 'end,' although this fact is now lost in the borborygmal mists that obscure so much of etymology.

"Reepah's concept was a simple one. He would return to Japan and teach a new spiritual practice, based on the mastery of a simple, natural process: farting. His students, he believed, would immediately see the joke he was playing on them, laugh, and free themselves from the limits imposed by their narrow cultural views. He would then be able to teach them true Buddhism.

"'But what if they do not get the joke?' asked Pin-Chee. 'What if they take this new spiritual science of farting seriously?'

"'I have thought of that. My own students may be too inclined to believe me and too polluted with cultural traditions to see this hoax, obvious though it is. But sooner or later, as the Zen of Farting is passed from generation to generation, someone is bound to realize that it is a joke— and expose my little farce. He will then lead his students into a new spiritual realization.'

"Pin-Chee had his doubts, but he kept them to himself. He helped his brother compose scriptures, instructions, and verses for his new religion, Zen. And he wished Reepah success as he sailed away, back to Japan. But, in setting down the story of Reepah Gud Wan's life and mission, Pin-Chee clearly sees the truth:

"'Reepah never returned to China; he spent

the rest of his days in Japan, preaching the power of farting. Not a soul, however, suspected that it was a joke; they eagerly embraced Zen as a new revelation. They began holding farting contests to see who could issue the purest, most spiritual flatus. One monk learned to perform musical tunes with his farts, and became a well-rewarded entertainer in the Emperor's court. This spawned the appearance of "fartists," flatulent musicians who traveled the countryside squeezing out the latest tunes. This led, as might be expected, to the ultimate desecration of Reepah's vision—the emergence of "the order of the Blue Flame," a troupe of gymnasts who would ignite their farts and perform acrobatics while sustaining the fireworks. Performed after nightfall, it never failed to bring down the house.

"'Reepah died, disappointed that his effort had backfired, but still clinging to the hope that the joke would eventually be recognized.'

"It is at this point that Pin-Chee's account ends. But a later ancestor added more information. At the time of Reepah Gud Wan's life, the main staple of the Japanese diet was beans, not rice. This fact greatly facilitated the practice of Zen, as farts came easily and frequently to even a novice disciple. But about two hundred years after Reepah died, there was a climatic change in the weather in Japan which brought in an unusual amount of rain. The soil became far too wet for beans, and most of the plants rotted in the ground before they had a chance to mature. The Japanese were forced to start cultivating rice, and it replaced beans as the staple of their diet.

"This change made farting much more difficult, to the point where even the Zen masters could not demonstrate some of the simplest precepts as taught by Reepah Gud Wan.

"But still no one could see it was a joke. Instead, they simply dropped the ritual and techniques of farting from the teachings of Zen, and left only the empty husks of Reepah's instructions. It became, in essence, the Zen of Nothing, instead of the Zen of Farting. It has remained thus ever since."

The narration then returned to Lett Wan Fli.

"The worst fears of Pin-Chee have now been realized. Twelve hundred years later, the joke has been lost, but Zen continues on, as though it were some kind of spiritual neutron bomb. It has become a part of the Japanese character, but not to anyone's advantage. Where is the Buddha in Zen? Where, even, is the fart in my ancestor's practical joke? As you say in America, it is 'gone with the wind.'

"Zen without farting is just a whole lot of emptiness. It is the moon without the sun, a river bed without water. It would be healthier and more spiritual to take a nap than practice Zen as it is today. I cannot understand why so many people are drawn to it. There is nothing spiritual in Zen. It is just a bad smell in the air—the extinction of the mind.

"What makes this situation even more serious is that Zen is no longer just a local problem on the islands of Japan. It has been exported to Europe and the United States, where it has been eagerly consumed by undiscriminating people. They need to be warned of the true nature of Zen—of the 'silent but violent' emptiness of this practice. Just because it has been practiced diligently for a thousand years does not make it spiritual, or even useful. It is a joke that can no longer squeeze out a punch line.

"I am not advocating putting the fart back into Zen, as I am sure you understand. Zen was designed to be a translucent technique, inviting its students to see through it—in a way, very much like the recent bestseller—what is its title?—The Cellophane Prophecy. I am a voice, crying in the wilderness: 'Wake up and smell the fart. If it stinks, don't make a religion out of it!'

"This is why I am sending this material to you. I have researched all of the publishers in America in the hopes of finding one that might be sympathetic to my story. But how could I trust today's publishers? By and large, they have all been deceived about the legitimacy of Zen themselves.

"Have you looked at bookstore shelves lately? Once it was just The Zen of Archery. Then it was Zen and the Art of Motorcycle Maintenance. Now it is The Zen of Everything Under the Sun—The Zen of Twiddling Your Thumbs, the Zen of Picking Your Nose, and the Zen of Tobacco Spitting.

"You alone seem capable of recognizing the truth. So, I appeal to you, sir—spread the word. Tell the world about the Zen of Farting. It is a story that has been in the making for twelve hundred years—but now the time is ripe to air it. Please do so, before it is too late!"

Naturally, this appeal caught my attention and sustained it. I have long believed that our Western society is too rigid and prudish in many of its attitudes, especially toward natural functions. Why are we so prissy when it comes to farting, belching, crapping, and pissing? The body needs to perform these functions many times a day. Indeed, medical science has learned that the healthy body needs to fart twenty times each day! But we consider it polite to repress our farts and belches, lest they offend others. As a result, the natural health processes of the body suffer.

A fart is actually no different than an exhaled breath—it just comes out the other end. Could we breathe without exhaling? Of course not; we would die. Should we live without farting? Nature says, "No." But we are taught from the earliest age that not only should we never fart, we should never even talk about it!

Musing in this way on this subject, I soon concluded that it would be a public service to publish Reepah Gud Wan's little manual. It might well expose the naturalness of farting to a group of people who could then break down existing social barriers. But I was concerned what the reaction from faithful practitioners of Zen would be. After all, the commentary supplied to me by Lett Wan Fli pretty much pulls the meditation rug out from underneath the serious Zen student.

I consulted a number of friends who were aficionados of Zen, and got more or less the reaction I expected. They repudiated every word of it. One went so far as to say: "I don't care if Zen did start with a fart. I don't bake air biscuits when I am practicing Zen, and it leads me to a wonderful state of consciousness. I'm filled with the most sublime emptiness. So, go ahead and print the book. It won't change my mind."

It was then that I realized that the narrowness and limitations that troubled Reepah in his day still exist twelve hundred years later—and actually draw people to Zen. So I stopped worrying about their reactions. I decided to publish the book. If readers get the point, fine. Those who do not will probably be found in Zen retreats.

As a public service for those readers who were taught to blush whenever they heard a word like "fart," I will briefly review a few euphemisms they may not know.

Farting is also known as:

> Baking an air biscuit.
> Cutting the cheese.
> Squeezing the breeze.
> Stepping on a duck.
> Beefing.
> Queefing.

Farts themselves are sometimes known as beefers, air biscuits, and floaters. Especially wicked farts are referred to as silent but deadly and silent but violent.

Obviously, Reepah Gud Wan did not use this slang in his teachings, nor did Pin-Chee Wan. They used words appropriate to their time and the Chinese dialect. Most of our modern phrases were supplied by Lett Wan Fli in his translation; occasionally, I have updated his choice of words to reflect modern idioms.

I cannot vouch for the authenticity of the text that follows, or the accuracy of its content. I am printing it because it was sent to me, and it makes sense. I leave it to each reader to decide, for him or her self, just what the meaning of it is.

As Reepah Gud Wan would probably have said: "Meaning? Truth? What is meaning? It is just truth concealed within a fart."

—*Carl Japikse, Publisher*

THE

WAY

OF THE

GOUDA

These are the teachings of Sri Reepah Gud Wan, a disciple of our Lord Gautama Buddha and a master of the spiritual practice of Zen, as set down by his brother and disciple, Pin-Chee Wan.

Reepah Gud Wan attained enlightenment in the following manner:

Growing up in a small village in China, the young Reepah was drawn to the life of asceticism and spiritual discovery. He left his father's home at the age of fourteen and travelled to India and Ceylon, where he studied with many teachers, but no masters. He became discouraged that he met so many people who called themselves Buddhists and teachers who had not achieved the enlightenment and wisdom of the Great One.

He was studying with his fifteenth teacher when the old man passed gas. In his spiritual journey, Reepah had been taught to observe everything in life and try to understand it. So he applied this lesson to the example at hand.

"Guru," he inquired, "what is the meaning of your flatulence?"

"Insolent lad," growled the teacher. "Farts have no meaning."

"But they must," Reepah insisted. "Everything in life has meaning. Everything in life has cause and effect. This is the law of karma."

"I eat beans, therefore I fart," growled the guru. "It is your karma to suffer through the stench obediently. It prepares you for life."

The young Reepah meditated on this teaching for many hours. At last, he understood: his guru did not know beans. He stood and picked up his meditation mat.

"Where are you going?" his guru asked. "You have not completed your lessons."

"Yes, I have," replied Reepah. "I have achieved enlightenment."

"Oh?" retorted the incredulous guru. "And what have you learned?"

"I have learned that a fart contains more insight and wisdom than your teachings," he said evenly. "The insight came through as clear as won ton soup:

"If you wanna be a buddha,

"You gotta cut the Gouda."

"What on earth does that mean?" the guru asked.

"What we call life is just as shallow and meaningless as a fart, which lasts a moment and then dissipates into the air from which it was born. When we die, our bodies become dust, just as a fart becomes air again.

In the same way, everything we hold dear likewise resolves into its original essence: values, principles, goals, and aspirations. If we take them seriously, we will suffer when they are stolen from us, just as the Lord Buddha taught. But if we see that they are all farts in the wind, and let them fly, then we can dwell in the original essence, which is fragrant and sweet, instead of the fart, which is not.

The guru did not understand a word of what Reepah said, but was impressed nonetheless. "You surely are enlightened," he muttered. "Go, with my blessing. I can teach you nothing more." Which was a true statement, since in fact, he had not taught Reepah anything to begin with.

Thus did Reepah Gud Wan
achieve enlightenment.

REEPAH'S FIRST STUDENT

When Reepah Gud Wan first journeyed to Japan to teach the techniques and rituals of the Zen of Farting, he was entertained by Lee-Ki Pee, the war lord in the region where Reepah had chosen to start his work. Lee-Ki Pee was a man of ferocious cruelty and rigid habits, and he did not like the idea of a Chinese monk setting up shop in his province. Nonetheless, he welcomed Reepah with all of the hospitality that would be expected.

"Tell me something about myself that I do not already know," said Lee-Ki, "and I will

reward you with a monastery and sixty hectares of land."

"Your life is as empty as a minute-old fart," replied Reepah Gud Wan pleasantly.

The war lord was outraged, and made little effort to control his vaunted temper. "What?" he screeched. "How dare you insult me. Who are you to call me an old fart! I should have you flogged, you miserable excuse for an unholy mongrel. I should have you executed!"

"I pray that you would," answered Reepah

Gud Wan, "as it would spare me much trouble."

"What are you babbling about?" demanded Lee-Ki.

"I would no longer have to trouble myself to speak with respect to you and others like you, people who think they know it all."

Lee-Ki was impressed by the courage of this teacher. "I am intrigued by your statements," he said. "Why do you think that I am an old fart with an empty life? I have everything a man could ever desire—five thousand soldiers, twenty-thousand peasants, sixty wives, and two hundred children. I am a man of immense wealth. I have bought the services of the best scholars, artists, philosophers, and astronomers. How is my life empty?"

"I hope you kill people better than you listen," said Reepah. "I did not call you an old fart, nor did I say your life was empty. I said it was as empty as a minute-old fart. Now, a minute-old fart is one that has largely dissipated into the air, just as your glory has spread throughout the lands that you control. It is rapidly becoming a memory—but a memory of what? From what does a fart proceed? Flatulence is a sign that you have just dined, and in all likelihood, dined well. A floater is a herald of satisfaction, an angel of contentment.

"But look at your life. Are you really contented? Or have you missed the main course? Your original question answers mine: you would not have asked me to tell you something you did not know unless you were well aware, in some deep recess of your soul, that you did not possess everything. You are not satisfied, milord. There is something missing in your life."

"And what is that?" the shogun demanded.

"The inner realities of life. You have your army, but you do not own its fierceness. You have many wives, but you do not rule their affection. You have peasants to labor for you, but you do not own their diligence. And so, in the one area where it counts, the Inner Court of Meaning, your life is as empty as a minute-old fart. You have the appearances of contentment, but you do not have its spirit."

"And how do I obtain this spirit of contentment?" inquired the war lord, hoping very much that it did not involve giving up his wealth and lands and power and slaves and becoming a humble monk.

"By learning to expel the perfect fart," replied Reepah Gud Wan.

Lee-Ki spat impatiently.

"And what is the perfect fart? Who can tell one fart from another?"

"If you could inhale only wisdom, and let it rule your life, you would eventually learn to express perfect judgment. If you study the Zen of Farting, the day will come when you will expel only perfect farts, pure and sweet to the senses. You will be content—and so will the rest of your household."

"You shall have your monastery, O learned one, and I shall be your pupil. All of my men shall be your students as well. We will learn to practice this Zen of Farting."

At that moment, the Master Reepah Gud Wan knew his plan was in serious jeopardy.

Emptiness

Listen to the wisdom of the Master Reepah Gud Wan:
Every human being farts. We also sing, eat, make love, work, and play. But of all of these activities, only farting truly represents the emptiness of human life. When we sing, we are preoccupied with the music and words. When we eat, we think about the food we are consuming. When we make love, we think about our partners and how desirable they are. When we work, we dwell on the demands of the job. When we play, we focus on the rules of the game.

But farting is. It does not require our conscious intent, or even our intelligent cooperation. Whenever we fart, therefore, we become free to be our own true self.

Unless, of course, we try to suppress the fart. Most of you have been raised in a society that suppresses its farts. It is viewed as impolite to fart in public. In this way, even the most unspoiled function of human living becomes corrupted by silly people, people who insist on telling you how to live your life.

When we suppress farts, we create something artificial, or shall I say, *fartificial,* out of a perfectly natural process. This is a sign of the degenerate nature of society.

Your whole life is filled with the fartificial.

The purpose of my teaching is to help you see the fartificial, and then eliminate it from your life, so that you may enter the Inner Court of Meaning.

When we fart, we cannot see it. Nor can we see meaning.

When we fart, the odor lasts a few seconds. When we touch meaning, or have a glimpse of it, our awareness likewise lasts only a few seconds.

To perceive meaning, you must look beyond your work and play, your duties and love making. You must transcend even your singing, no matter how angelic it might be.

To the beginning disciple, meaning may seem no more concrete than a fading fart. But it is there. It is your job to find it, claim it, and seize it.

Keep this in mind: there are two possible conditions in human life. Fart and No-Fart. The first describes the freedom to let one fly. If you follow it with your mind, it may eventually lead you into even more intangible realms, the Inner Court of Meaning. But No-Fart is the state of human life as it usually is—a prison of suppressed energy, bloated with a tragically false sense of its self-importance.

You must learn to distinguish between the Fart and the No-Fart. In doing so, however, you will estrange yourself from others—and the rest of society. You may even be condemned for what you know to be true.

The difference between Fart and No-Fart is the difference between wholeness and emptiness. Only the man who has learned to give up his emptiness can ever become whole. This is the Way of the Gouda.

Each fart, used as a focus for your meditations, will guide you. It will lead you from the concrete into the subtle—and then to the sublime.

There you will behold Truth, and you will then know that the things of earth are all fartificial.

When you have done that, you will no longer need a fart to guide you.

You will know who you are.

You will no longer be empty.

You will be full of it.

Fart and No-Fart

Master, how can we learn to distinguish between the Fart and the No-Fart?

Eat beans.

I do not understand.

Of course not. That is why you are my pupil.

We must eat in order to live, is that not true? The staple of our diet is beans, am I correct? When we eat, we become full. We are satisfied. We fart in order to release the joy of our contentment. If you meditate on the joy which is expressed by farting, you will arrive at an understanding of the meaning of joy.

But you must not therefore conclude that farts contain joy. They do not. They stink.

Think more deeply, my son. Just hours after we have eaten, we are hungry again. We must eat another meal, so that our contentment may return. Our unborn farts need this fuel.

Contentment that is based on our latest meal will fade quickly. Contentment based on any of the pleasures of the earth must be constantly replenished. But there is a kind of contentment that endures forever—the contentment of the Inner Court of Meaning.

When you base your contentment on food, riches, comfort, and sex, you always need more. You can never be satisfied for more than a few hours. You remember what you have known in the past, and become dissatisfied with what you imagine you are stuck with in the present.

The artist and poet find contentment in more subtle things—in the refined nature of ideas and beauty. This is a step in the right direction. But even they are usually trapped in the fartificial, and unwilling to give it up. They color their

perceptions of beauty and truth with their own prejudices and assumptions. They are still trapped in the illusions of the earth. They take their work too seriously. They forget to fart.

To become perfectly free, as free as the fart, you must seek out and find the sublime—the invisible, the intangible, the infinite. Then your talents and affections can expand and fill the whole world, just as a fart fills an entire room.

You will then realize that of all of the things of earth, only the Fart is real—because it can lead us to meaning. Everything else is just No-Fart.

This is why I say, "Eat beans." They will remind you of how impermanent self-gratification is. A few hours later, you are hungry again and must eat more beans. Always more beans!

For far too many people, all that can be said of them when they die is this: they ate beans.

That is not the Way of the Gouda. Live your life, my son, so that when you die, people will say of you:

"He ate beans, but he learned to fart."

Zen Mind, Never Mind

Listen to the teachings of Master Reepah Gud Wan:

Farts are projected from the rectum.

Feelings are projected from our reactions.

Thoughts are projected from our reason.

Which will lead us most quickly to the Inner Court of Meaning?

An unpleasant fart disappears in moments.

An unpleasant feeling can make you bitter for a lifetime.

A depressing thought can imprison you in self-pity and make you incapable of entering the Inner Court of Meaning.

Pessimistic thoughts can entrap whole nations and races of people.

The Zen of Farting teaches you that you are meant to be a master of your farts. Suppressing them does not lead to mastery; it leads only into the land of No-Fart. It is the state of illusion. You must recognize that farts lead you to freedom. Then you can find the contentment of the Inner Court of Meaning.

The Zen of Farting likewise teaches you that you are meant to be a master of your feelings and reactions. Envy, bitterness, anger, and hate are worse than the most wicked fart ever. And they do not dissipate. You carry them with you wherever you go, polluting other people—and the earth itself—with your fetid aura of jealousy or ire.

This is the Prison of Hurt Feelings. Most members of humanity are presently inmates.

The Zen of Farting also teaches you that you are meant to be master of your thoughts. Ideas and inspiration are the gifts of the gods to each of us. They must be welcomed with hospitality and made to feel at home in our heads. Would you remove all of the furniture from your living room before entertaining a cousin or friend? Of course not. Would you refuse to serve your guests tea? Of course not. Would you sit there silently, or ignore them? Of course not. You would entertain them.

We must entertain ideas in the same way. Do not pay attention to those people who insist that we must empty the mind in order to discover meaning. Having started with an empty mind, they never notice the difference. But we must sharpen the mind, like an ax, so it can cut through the nonsense taught by people who do not know.

The problem with the mind is that it is often filled with silly notions, such as this one about the virtue of an empty mind. Try telling a wealthy man that it is a virtue to empty his bank account! See what his response is. Silly notions distort our thinking.

Too much doubt is a silly use of the mind.

Too much rigidity is a silly use of the mind.

Too much emphasis on what is wrong in life is a silly use of the mind.

To practice Zen, we must stop abusing the mind with silly thoughts. We must not, however, stop using the mind.

If you try to stop using the mind, then never mind, because your thoughts will not be worth a fart. At the same time, you must defend your mind, lest it be bombarded by silliness. Just as a mother will say to a child "Never mind," when the child asks something it does not need to know, the student of Zen will say "Never mind" when confronted with silly thoughts.

It is for this reason that in the Zen of Farting, we say:

"Zen Mind, Never Mind."

BE STILL, MY FART

When I practice Zen, I am unable to keep distractions out of my mind. How can I still my mind, Master?

You are not to still the mind, my son. I never suggested that you still your mind.

You said to sharpen it like an ax. What would you use the ax for, but to kill distractions?

The mind is a noble part of your potential, my son. It does not create distractions; it exposes them. When given the authority to do so, it expels them. Never let anyone tell you not to use your mind, or encourage you to still it. A stilled mind is a dead mind, a mind that cannot be revived.

When I quote the Zen aphorism, "Zen mind,

Never mind," I am not suggesting that you should never have a mind. What foolishness! I am giving you a key to gaining mastery over the distractions and interruptions created by our feelings. I am telling you: do not let the clarity of your thinking and understanding be dragged down by the silliness of sentiment and emotion. Pay no heed to such reactiveness: it is nonsense.

If I interrupted you when you were meditating and cried, "Your pants are on fire," how would you respond?

The disciple thought a long time, and then said:

Never mind?

The Master beamed. "Exactly. Why?"

I do not know.

Then listen. There are two possibilities. Either your pants are on fire, or I am wrong. If your pants are on fire, you should know through your own direct perception. You do not need me to tell you. You should therefore say, "Never

mind." If they are not on fire, then I am misleading you. You should once again say, "Never mind."

Of course, if your pants are on fire, then it is not enough just to become aware of this fact. You must also understand why. In all likelihood, you have emitted an especially combustible fart, and it ignited your pants.

Most importantly of all, you must take action. You must remove your flaming pants as quickly as possible and throw them in a bucket of water.

These are the three elements of correct thought:

1. Right perception.
2. Right understanding.
3. Right action.

Most people, however, do not teach their minds these noble truths. They are guided by their feelings and emotions, which ensnare them in the Prison of Hurt Feelings. If their pants caught on fire, they would immediately place the blame on someone else, probably the monastery itself. They would likewise criticize God for allowing this misfortune to happen. They would next feel shame that this misfortune happened to them. Finally, they would pretend that the whole episode never happened. They would actually deny the original fart that set their pants aflame.

These are the distractions we must train ourselves to "never mind." Unless, of course, you want to go through life with your ass on fire.

ZEN PRACTICE

Listen to the wisdom of the Master Reepah Gud Wan:

It takes practice to master the way of the Gouda. As you sit in meditation, allow a fart to expel itself naturally.

Contemplate it.

How did the fart originate?

How did it work its way out of the stomach, through the intestine, to where it could be expelled from the rectum?

What motivated this fart?

What, in essence, was this fart?

Where did it go?

What is it now?

It will take many long sessions to be able to

answer each of these questions correctly. You must learn to let the fart you have expelled lead you into the more subtle realms of awareness. Should you lose your concentration, you can renew it by cutting loose another fart.

You may laugh at any time during this process. If you wish, feel free to laugh out loud. Such laughter is a sign that you are being set free, and it will inspire other students who might hear it to redouble their efforts.

On the other hand, you are *not* encouraged to cry, even if you encounter guilt, shame, or cruelty within yourself. Crying traps you within the Prison of Hurt Feelings. We are trying to liberate you. We are trying to ascend to the Inner Court of Meaning. This is why we fart— and laugh.

The Zen of Farting is not to be undertaken seriously. It is the way to perfect contentment, perfect joy. Do not be intimidated into being serious. Laugh. Fart. Enjoy yourself.

It is by contemplating your own ability to fart that you set yourself free from the Prison of Hurt Feelings. When you can laugh at a fart, can you not also laugh at the silliness of being embarrassed, or feeling guilty, or carrying a grudge, or wanting to harm someone? Can you not laugh at taking the taboos of society seriously or following the repressed codes of other people?

Laugh. Life is nothing but a fart in the breeze, until you follow your fart and see where it goes.

After sufficient practice, the day will arrive when you can say, as others before you have said:

If you wanna be free
You gotta cut the brie.

Silent But Violent

O

I do not understand how farting can help me temper my anger. This seems absurd.

Life *is* absurd, unless you understand the simplicity of the fart.

Farting is a natural process of elimination. After eating, gas builds in our system during the bacterial actions of digestion. These gases seek to escape, to return to the air, which is their natural element. As they break free from the colon and pass out the rectum, they produce flatulence. Whether accompanied by a loud noise or not, our farts emit strong odors.

We call this process "cutting the cheese,"

because many cheeses also emit strong odors, when you cut into them.

Unfortunately, the emotions do not have such a built-in safety valve. Most people nurture themselves on the wrong kind of emotional food. They grieve when confronted with death. They grow angry when exposed to imperfection or indifference. They carry grudges when they believe that they have been harmed. They worry, even when there is nothing to fret about. These pent-up feelings are truly "silent but violent."

Our emotions seek to expel these toxins, just as our digestive tract cleanses itself by farting. But there is no way the emotions can do this automatically. An angry person can lose his or her temper and erupt like a volcano, but this does not expel the toxins. It just exercises them. He or she is still as much an angry, spiteful person after venting this anger as before.

You may think that I exaggerate, but as I look around, I can see the mounting toxins of the emotions of every person. In each case, I pray that they may learn to use their God-given capacity to fart to vent these bilious energies before they are destroyed by them.

You see, anger is worse than the foulest fart ever laid down by man or woman. Depression hangs in your aura like the fart that never dies. And some of the worst emotions of all are the "silent but deadly" ones—the resentment that is never voiced, the irritation that is never expressed. All of these noxious gases of sentiment and desire build up in your emotions, until you become a walking stink bomb.

How do I know this? Do I practice clairvoyance? No, I practice clairsniffience. I sniff out your character, and believe me, the evidence is usually quite strong.

Learn from the example God has given you, my child. As you meditate upon your farts, let them do double duty for you. In addition to letting each fart be a guide to more subtle levels of awareness, use it to expel a portion of your emotional poisons as well. Let every fart flush out some of your anger, your irritation, your impatience, your grief, or your sadness, and you will shortly be a much healthier, sane person.

In short, my son, the answer to your question is "blowing in the wind." How much you suffer all depends on just where you stand.

ZEN MEDITATION

Listen to the wisdom of Master Reepah Gud Wan:

There are three steps in meditation:

1. Indifference.
2. Absorption.
3. Identification.

In the Zen of Farting, we do not meditate by staring at a candle, or by contemplating the picture of our guru. We break wind, and then follow our fart wherever it take us.

Our first impressions of the fart remind us of the need for indifference. To penetrate the meaning of flatulence, we must first of all smell it. The Zen of Farting is not an exercise in self-deception. Farts stink. My farts stink. So will yours—and so will those of the person next to you, if you are meditating together. This is one reason why we do not usually practice group meditations in the Zen of Farting.

It is not just in regard to floaters that we need to practice indifference, of course. The fart merely reminds us of the larger reality. Each beginning Farter brings with him a great deal of baggage—expectations, fears, doubts, worries, illusions, and attachments. He is controlled by everyone and everything around him, rather than by himself. Before he can meditate, he must learn to become indifferent toward all of the things he has previously cared about—or reacted to. He does not need to eliminate them from his life—this is the Zen of Farting, not the Zen of Crapping—but he must not let them control him any longer. He must liberate himself from his own stink.

If you can meditate in a closed room that

smells like a chicken coop, you are well on your way to learning indifference.

The second stage of learning to meditate is absorption. We must attune our mind to become absorbed in the Inner Court of Meaning. But Meaning is invisible, and you have no experience in interacting with it. You do not even know where to look for it.

This is the point of following your farts, as they dissipate into the air. They become subtler and subtler, until they are hardly there at all. But we come to realize, through this practice, that they have not actually disappeared. They have just resolved into their component elements. We can therefore focus our attention on these component elements. Then comes a momentous realization. While the smell has dissipated, the fart still lives! It has just returned to its original state. It has been absorbed by the air.

We, too, want to be absorbed—not by our farts, or even by the air, but in the Inner Court of Meaning. But we must train our minds to work in subtle, and even sublime ways, in order to be absorbed in this way. And so we fart.

Absorption in meaning allows us to identify with our innermost essence. You are presently identified with your body and your ego. As a result, you are weak and immature. There is great strength, love, and wisdom in your innermost essence, but you do not know how to identify with these qualities. As a result, you identify only with what is wrong with your life, and this induces suffering.

As we fart and meditate upon our air biscuits, we realize we are not the farts. We produced the farts, but we are greater than they are. Some beginners do try to identify with their farts, but this is an error, unless you are very old, and therefore an Old Fart.

Laughter, as you remember, is an important part of the Zen of Farting.

We fart, but farting does not describe who we are.

It does not take any talent to fart. Any idiot can do it—and in fact, an idiot may well be able to squeeze one out better than you. So do not identify with your talents either.

Neither is farting any great accomplishment. A dog or a cat can fart every bit as well as a man. So do not identify with your achievements.

Farting is a natural act. It is a sign of the wisdom of nature itself. Can you imagine life without farting? Where would all that gas go? It would build up in your bowels like a balloon, until you exploded.

By contemplating identity in this way, with the help of your farts, you will eventually come to realize who you are.

You are.

Nothing more, nothing less.

It is merely incidental that you fart, or live in Japan, or fish for a living, or eat beans.

You are.

You know.

You love.

You act.

If you eat enough beans, you fart.

Knowing this, you can meditate.

And, in time, you may even reach Nirvana— the state of the fartless fart.

FREE TO FART

Master, I understand the value of cutting the cheese in meditation. And I am comfortable with this technique as long as I am at the monastery. But when I go home, and have to meditate in the small room I share with my three brothers, I feel guilty. It is as though I am imposing my will on theirs when I fart. How can I handle my guilt?

I am the Master Reepah Gud Wan, not Dear Crabby! You should be able to sort out these petty problems on your own. Nonetheless, I will answer your inquiry.

Guilt can be a short route into the Prison of Hurt Feelings.

If you have committed a crime, guilt is a good thing. It nags at you to recognize your error and go straight. If you have hurt someone else, guilt likewise scolds you until you apologize and make amends.

But to feel guilty about queefing a few air biscuits! This is self-destructive. You might as well feel guilty about the silly demands your mother-in-law makes on you, or the crude attempts of your neighbors to shame or humiliate you because you think differently than they.

If you are uncomfortable farting in the presence of your brothers, go sit in a shed to meditate. If your brothers are uncomfortable because you fart, take pity upon them. They have not yet found the liberation that comes from letting an air biscuit fly.

In the Zen of Farting, we have a saying: "A man who has never farted is a blind man trying to see through his nose."

Farting teaches us to tread the way without carrying the burden of guilt.

O, free to fart! Free at last!

FLOWER POWER

Listen to the wisdom of Master Reepah Gud Wan:

You may have been taught by others that each meditation session should begin by placing fresh flowers and incense on an altar in your meditation room or nook, in honor of your guru.

Your guru does not need honor. Either he already has honor, or he should not be a guru. If he demands that you honor and pay homage to him, he must not have as much enlightenment as he asserts.

Nonetheless, it is an excellent idea to bring fresh flowers and incense to your special meditation area—not to use before or during your meditation, but to use after you have finished your contemplations.

The more fragrant the flowers are, the more they will tend to mask any unpleasing, lingering odors. They will also help to refresh your nostrils, which by now will be fatigued from sniffing farts.

Some of the best flowers to use for this purpose would be lavender, honeysuckle, and hyacinth. The rose will also do exceptionally well in a pinch.

It is also a thoughtful gesture to insert a small sachet of cleansing aromas into the seat of your pants after you have finished meditating.

Burning incense is another excellent way to dispose of the aftermath of an exceptionally intense meditation. I personally recommend Musk.

But remember, do not use either of these aids until your meditation is complete. It is of vital importance that you absorb the full bouquet of your farts.

POSTURES

Listen to the wisdom of Master Reepah Gud Wan:

In India, there are many postures for meditation. They call these postures *asanas*. The hardest of all is the full lotus.

I do not advocate these postures, because it is hard to fart properly when twisted up like a pretzel. I therefore recommend that you meditate in a kneeling position, with your legs tucked behind you and

your buttocks slightly raised above the heels of your feet. Then, when you break wind, the fart will be expelled swiftly out behind you, well preserved and forceful. This will enable you to contemplate the fart in its fullness and richness.

Once the fart is on the fly, then you can gently rock back and rest the buttocks on your heels, until it is time to cut a new one. In this way, your knees will not tire.

This type of meditation obviously requires a meditation mat upon which to kneel. Only the knees need touch the mat. Do not sit on the mat under any circumstances, lest it become soiled by the accidental "hard fart."

Some beginners experience difficulty in staying awake while meditating. This is one of the advantages of the Zen of Farting. If you sense that you are beginning to drift into a slumber, just lay down a fresh fart. That will wake you up—and probably the novice next to you as well.

LEVITATION

Master, the explosive force of my meditation was so great that it actually lifted me off of my mat. Was I levitating?

No, you were farting.

It is not uncommon for meditators in the Zen of Farting to become so proficient in the Way of the Gouda that each fart actually propels them off of their mat. It looks as if they are hopping about the room. Fart-Hop. Fart-Hop. They are like a bunch of jumping beans, which perhaps they are.

This is not levitation. Levitation occurs as a result of absorption into the Inner Court of Meaning. It represents total mastery over the earth. You will be fortunate if you can gain mastery over your farts, let alone the fundamental principles of physics.

It is fun to hop, but it is not levitation. If you want to hop, go play games with small children. If you want enlightenment, stay here and break wind.

And if ever some swami in a sheet comes along and says that he will teach you how to levitate, introduce him to the Zen of Farting.

BREATHING

What about deep breathing, Master? Isn't that a part of all meditation practices?

There is no deep breathing in the Zen of Farting, my child. Have you ever smelled an air biscuit? Do you really want to fill your lungs with it?

Some beginners actually wear a veil for the first week or so.

The breath that we inhale is a lovely symbol for the spirit of God. As you inhale, you are not only bringing oxygen into your lungs, but you are also charging your aura with prana.

But the breath we inhale is no more spiritual than the breath we exhale. Each is just a breath.

Both are a necessary part of the cycle of life. So is rectal gas.

In the Zen of Farting, we concentrate on our farts, rather than our breath. As our farts dissolve back into the air from whence they came, we learn many spiritual truths.

In many societies, the priests still invoke their gods by sacrificing a lamb or a cock on the holy altar. In the Zen of Farting, our queefs become the offertories that lift our awareness to more subtle realms.

If you want to practice meditation by using techniques of deep breathing, then by all means do so. But let me give you one final word of advice as you leave my monastery:

Don't practice your deep breathing downwind from the rest of us.

Zen Diet

O

Listen to the wisdom of the Master Reepah Gud Wan:

Diet is a very important part of the Zen of Farting. Without the proper imbalance in what you eat, you may never fart. It is therefore of utmost importance to eat foods that your system cannot wholly digest, and ones that will result in an appropriate volume of gas. It is also helpful to eat those foods that will stink to high heaven when we fart, for that is where we want to go.

Your salvation, in other words, lies with beans and other starches and legumes. For some people, milk is also helpful.

As the ancient practitioners of Zen chant before each meal time:

Beans, beans, the mystical meal
The more you eat, the more bloated you feel.
Beans for our appetizer,
Beans for dessert,
Beans for our main course
Will keep us alert.
Beans in the skillet, beans in tureens—
We can eat anything so long as it's beans.

Some people believe that it is also a good idea to gulp down your food, thereby inhaling large quantities of air as you eat. I cannot vouch for this practice, however.

It is also very important to prepare the beans with the right attitude. A conscientious Zen cook will handle each bean reverently, imagining in his mind the wonderful farts that lie untapped within its little body. But take care: the wise Zen chef does not let his beans soak in water, because that will lessen their unique character— their capacity to give people gas.

Cooking Your Beans

Master, how will I know when I have achieved enlightenment?

You'll know it when the god of thunder farts.

Enlightenment is the state of full identification with the Inner Court of Meaning. It represents the highest state of meditation, although most people who meditate never reach enlightenment.

To help you recognize when you have reached enlightenment, I have developed a series of cute phrases that have no literal meaning. They can only be understood by someone who possesses full enlightenment. I call these phrases "koans," the ancient Senzar word for "beans." Since the Zen of Farting owes so much to beans, I thought they should be given this honor.

A whole set of koans is known as "a kettle of beans." In part, the work of meditation is therefore a process of "cooking your beans."

For this reason, the question we are considering here could be restated: "How will I know when my beans are cooked?"

The most famous koan answers this question: "You'll know it when the god of thunder farts."

This is how this bean originated:

I was walking along the road on a sunny day in my native China when suddenly my reveries were interrupted by a horrendous fart. I suppose it was just an ox in the field finding relief, but it sounded to me like a thunderclap. At that precise moment, I hit upon an answer I had been seeking all afternoon. I therefore said to myself: "My beans are done! The god of thunder has farted!"

This is the mystery of the thunderclap, as we call it. It is also the first koan. By reflecting on this koan in your meditations, you will begin to see the shallowness and superficiality of ordinary human life, and the need for something of much greater value.

Here is another koan: "Once the sideboard is empty, how can you cut the cheese?"

And a third: "If a lumberjack farts in the woods, does a tree fall?"

Beans come in all sizes and shapes. For example: "Floats like a butterfly, stinks like a bean." This is the bean of choice of students applying the Zen of Farting to archery, or farchery, as we refer to it.

And then there is the philosophic conundrum: "How do you define what the meaning of 'is' is?"

My favorite, though, is the following: "What is the sound of no one farting?"

THE FARTING OX

O

The role of the farting ox in the story of the cooked beans, as described by the Master Reepah Gud Wan, has led to a special tradition in the Zen of Farting. There is no better omen of good fortune than to pass a flatulent ox. Conversely, there is no worse omen than to be caught behind a flatulent ox!

Throughout the ages, many Zen masters have embellished this simple story, each adding a key insight into the mastery of Zen.

Master Wat A Piu was the first to add a commentary:

The rains fall. They dampen the silage that the ox will eat. The moist hay begins to ferment. When the ox dines, fireworks will ensue. Good fortune is assured.

Clearly, the rains refer to the great ideas and inspirations of life, and their capacity to precipitate into our lives and awaken our minds, if we are well-prepared. In this way, society is "fermented" to be receptive to new approaches to living. As obvious as this metaphor is, it has nonetheless been trivialized by some experts as setting a precedent for imbibing alcoholic beverages. But the Zen of Farting needs no artificial stimulus. We get high on farts.

Master See Mi Pee added this:

I smell the farts, but cannot see the ox.

In this brilliant observation, the idea that the ox may be a link to transcendental levels of reality is first hinted.

His disciple, Queef Ree Leaf, went a step further:

The ox has run off, leaving us only with farts. Good fortune increases.

Queef Ree Leaf could really cook his beans! In these few words, he takes the ox out of a personal context of individual enlightenment, and transforms the image into a metaphor for human life. The ox now portrays universal life— the Inner Court of Meaning. We cannot possibly know much of anything about universal life—like the ox, it is not part of our personal landscape. It is here, yet not here. But even if we cannot study the ox, we can contemplate its farts, and so we are blessed. We can follow them throughout the universe.

This insight was truly a cosmic thunderclap. Knowing that he could not outdo the cosmic insight of Queef Ree Leaf, the next great master of the Zen of Farting, Flow Tin Wan, took a whole new approach to the ox story. He invented a bean:

Has the ox been harnessed?

It was many generations before this question was suitably answered. The reply came from a young student of the Zen of Farting. One day, having squeezed out a good one, he suddenly stood up from his meditation mat and announced:

It is our farts that harness the ox.

The teacher instantly recognized that this was the correct answer to a question that had stumped great minds for centuries. It was succinct, it was poignant. It had the air of truth.

"You have done it, my son. You have completed the farting ox cycle. How did it happen?"

"I don't know," stammered the puzzled disciple. "I had just farted when I suddenly beheld a vision of our great master, Reepah Gud Wan.

He was laughing his head off, muttering something about stupid people never getting a joke. Then he said to me, quite clearly: 'Our own farts harness the ox,' and broke down laughing again."

"This is indeed a marvel," said the teacher, who actually did not know beans. "Laughter is a great omen. Good things are in store for you."

Later that day, the boy was killed by a rampaging ox, who was not in the least deterred by a farting lad. Which reminds us once again: never assume that the Inner Court of Meaning is here in the physical. You are apt to be gored by a pissed off ox.

Partial Farts

The war lord Lee-Ki Pee came to the Master Reepah Gud Wan one afternoon and asked for an audience.

"My soldiers do not have time to sit all day cutting farts. They need time to practice their archery and kill defenseless people. And yet I most assuredly do want them to learn of your wisdom. How can this be accomplished?"

"It is an interesting question, Lee-Ki," replied the Master Reepah Gud Wan. "There is no substitute for a proper regimen of farting. Nonetheless, our rigorous practice can be adapted to accommodate the special needs of your soldiers.

We can modify the program. I shall call this system for warriors 'Partial Farts.'"

"Ah so," said Lee-Ki.

Thus was born the great tradition of Partial Farts. When an archer is standing with his bow, facing the target, he does not have time to kneel down on a meditation mat, assume a proper degree of indifference, and then cut a good one. So he must learn to bake his biscuits standing up. Just before each shot, he lets one fly. Then he lets his arrow fly. The fart guides his arrow to the bull's-eye.

Reepah Gud Wan asked an archer one day what his goal was. "To hit the bull's-eye," replied the archer.

"No, no, no," responded Reepah Gud Wan. "That is not right at all. You are thinking about archery, not farting. You must become absorbed in your partial fart, and let it lead you. Then you will shoot truly. Watch."

The Master Reepah Gud Wan picked up the

student's bow, notched an arrow, drew back his bowstring, cut loose a thunderous fart, closed his eyes, spun himself around, and—with his eyes still closed—shot the arrow. It hit the dead center of the bull's-eye.

Lee-Ki Pee happened to witness this incredible demonstration. He hurried over. "Where did you learn to shoot arrows like that?" he asked.

"Learn?" replied the master Reepah Gud Wan. "I have never shot a bow and arrow before in my life. But I was not shooting arrows. I was farting. In that, I have a measure of expertise."

As this story spread, warriors of all kinds—not just archers—lined up to learn the Zen of Farting, or the Zen of Farchery, as they called it. There were practitioners of karate and judo and all kinds of strange systems of maiming and killing others. They all went through the paces of Partial Farts. And they learned the solemn secret of success in all of these practices:

"When you come face to face with your enemy, and are both bowing in salutation, turn the other cheek and let one fly. The stink will disable him for a moment, allowing you to get in the first shot or kick or chop. Victory will be yours."

Strange as it may seem, a new group of samurai, or warriors, emerged as a result of Reepah Gud Wan's Partial Farts training: sumo wrestlers. Wrestling had been a popular sport in Japan for as long as history records, as is true in virtually every other country as well. But under the tutelage of Partial Farts, the wrestlers discovered something very important:

The more massive they became in bulk and hulk, the more powerfully they could expel a fart and disable their opponent. So, even at the price of agility and speed, they began to gorge themselves, so that they would become extremely fat.

The practice worked out even better than anticipated. The new breed of wrestlers bounced around the wrestling circle, raising their legs to gain maximum velocity and impact with their methane missiles. In fact, it was at this time that the expression "wiping the floor with your opponent" came into being.

Once the fart was lost from the practice of Zen, and all of the Partial Farts—due to the bean crop failure—the reason why sumo wrestlers grew fat slowly faded into obscurity. But the fat remains even today, as a silent but violent tribute to the long forgotten Fart.

THE

BLUE
QUEEF

RECORD

瑞巴格王大師在
自己村莊深思

[HSR]

The Blue Queef Record is a collection of the most prominent verses and catechisms in the long tradition of the Zen of Farting. Some of these sacred verses are reprinted here. It is clear from these few examples that the Zen of Farting was taken quite seriously by those who practiced it, and no one to this date, in the West as well as the East, has ever suspected the practical joke played upon them by the Master Reepah Gud Wan, in the hope of loosening up their cultural habits and outlooks.

A SONG

◯

I'd like to teach the world to queef
    In true cacaphony;
So eat some beans, sit on a duck,
    And squeeze out "middle C."

A MANTRAM

◯

Vast is the fart of liberation,
Emerging from my putrefaction—
    Leading to illumination;
We contemplate through our olfaction.

A BENEDICTION

◯

May all your farts be loud and swift,
    And send you on your way
To be absorbed in the Fragrant Whiff
    And Nature's Way obey.

FARTS

I think that I cannot impart
An invocation like a fart.

A fart escapes into the air
To float sedately—everywhere.

A fart's a messenger from me
For everyone to smell, not see.

Expelled with force, a fart extends
Beyond the pale where vision ends,

And sails into the next dimension
To liberate from strife and tension

All those who toil and moil below:
Where even heroes brave can't go.

Such farts are made for you and me,
Arise! Become all you can be.

THE SIX PERFECTIONS

○

1. Stench.
2. Velocity.
3. Longevity.
4. Loudness.
5. Impact.
6. Vastness.*

---

* Some experts point out that in the case of the Zen of Farting, this perfection should be "half-vastness," in tribute to the origin of all good things.